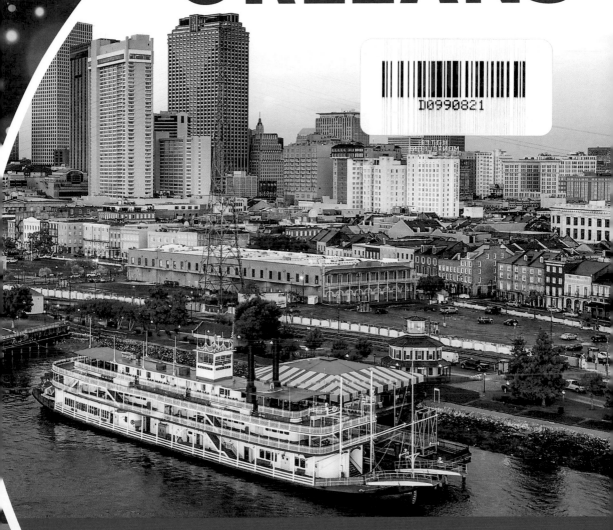

ICONIC AMERICA

NEW ORLEANS

BY MICHAEL DECKER

CONTENT CONSULTANT
Mary Niall Mitchell, PhD
Professor of History
University of New Orleans

Core Library

An Imprint of Abdo Publishing
abdobooks.com

Cover image: The steamboat *Natchez* docks near the
French Quarter in New Orleans.

abdobooks.com

Published by Abdo Publishing, a division of ABDO, PO Box 398166, Minneapolis, Minnesota 55439. Copyright © 2020 by Abdo Consulting Group, Inc. International copyrights reserved in all countries. No part of this book may be reproduced in any form without written permission from the publisher. Core Library™ is a trademark and logo of Abdo Publishing.

Printed in the United States of America, North Mankato, Minnesota
092019
012020

 THIS BOOK CONTAINS RECYCLED MATERIALS

Cover Photo: Kevin Ruck/Shutterstock Images
Interior Photos: Kevin Ruck/Shutterstock Images, 1; Sean Pavone/Shutterstock Images, 4–5, 28–29; Chuck Wagner/Shutterstock Images, 6, 45; Travel View/Shutterstock Images, 9, 43; Rainer Lesniewski/Shutterstock Images, 10; Sophia Germer/AP Images, 12–13; North Wind Picture Archives, 14; Red Line Editorial, 18; Richard Maschmeyer/robertharding/Newscom, 20–21; akg–images/Newscom, 23; H. Armstrong Roberts/ClassicStock/Alamy, 25; Ben Shahn/Everett Historical/Shutterstock Images, 31; AP Images, 33; Jeffrey Ufberg/WireImage/Getty Images, 36–37

Editor: Maddie Spalding
Series Designer: Claire Vanden Branden

Library of Congress Control Number: 2019942102

Publisher's Cataloging-in-Publication Data

Names: Decker, Michael, author.
Title: New Orleans / by Michael Decker
Description: Minneapolis, Minnesota : Abdo Publishing, 2020 | Series: Iconic America | Includes online resources and index.
Identifiers: ISBN 9781532190926 (lib. bdg.) | ISBN 9781532176777 (ebook)
Subjects: LCSH: New Orleans (La.)--History--Juvenile literature. | Louisiana--History--Juvenile literature. | French Quarter (New Orleans, La.)--Juvenile literature. | Jazz--Louisiana--New Orleans--History and criticism--Juvenile literature. | Bourbon Street (New Orleans, La.)--Juvenile literature.
Classification: DDC 917.633--dc23

CONTENTS

EXPLORING THE CITY

Tina and her family are walking in the French Quarter of New Orleans, Louisiana. In the main square, they see the historic Saint Louis Cathedral. The family then visits the Cabildo museum. The Cabildo acted as the city hall of New Orleans from 1799 to 1853. At the museum, they learn about Louisiana's history.

After exploring the museum, Tina and her family move on to Pirate's Alley. This famous walkway is also in the French Quarter. They stop by the Faulkner House. This house was named after author William Faulkner.

The Saint Louis Cathedral was originally built in 1727. It was rebuilt after a fire in 1794.

Jazz musicians often perform on the streets of New Orleans.

Faulkner lived there in 1925. Some of his writing was inspired by his time in New Orleans.

In the afternoon, Tina and her family are ready for a snack. They wait in line at Café du Monde. They order milk and beignets. Beignets are square French doughnuts covered in powdered sugar.

The family's last stop is the riverfront path known as the Moonwalk. This path runs next to the Mississippi River. They see musicians playing jazz music. Large ships move along the river. An old steamboat called the *Natchez* cruises past. Music from a calliope, or ship's organ, comes from the steamboat.

CITY OF CULTURES

The French Quarter in New Orleans dates back hundreds of years. It was the first neighborhood in the city. Different cultures have shaped what the French Quarter looks like today.

THE MISSISSIPPI RIVER

The Mississippi River starts in Minnesota. It flows from the northern United States down to the South. The river ends just south of New Orleans. From there, it flows into the Gulf of Mexico. People use the river's ports in New Orleans to export goods such as grain and soybeans. The river connects New Orleans to the rest of the United States and to the Gulf of Mexico. It is an important means of shipping and transportation.

New Orleans is in southeast Louisiana. It is the largest city in the state. In 2018, nearly 400,000 people lived in New Orleans. The city is known for its rich history. The city's residents have come from many different places.

Native Americans were the area's original occupants. Louisiana is home to several Native American tribes. These include the Chitimacha Tribe, the Coushatta Tribe, and the Tunica-Biloxi Indian Tribe. Choctaw Native Americans also live in the state.

Many of the buildings in the French Quarter were inspired by French and Spanish architecture.

French settlers founded New Orleans in 1718. The city became part of the Spanish Empire in 1763. Enslaved Africans built the city in the 1700s and 1800s. The United States took control of New Orleans in the 1800s. Today, French and Spanish cultures are still part of the city. New Orleans also has a large African American population. Many people of mixed African, French, or Spanish descent live in the city too. They identify themselves as Creoles. The city is well known for its Creole food.

NEW ORLEANS
MAP

This map shows the neighborhoods and suburbs of New Orleans. The colored areas are in the city, and the gray areas are suburbs. Which areas are the biggest? Is there anything that surprises you about this map?

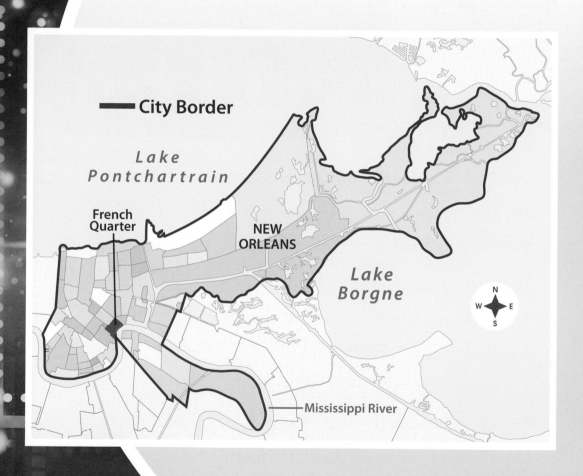

— City Border

Lake Pontchartrain

French Quarter

NEW ORLEANS

Lake Borgne

N
W E
S

Mississippi River

CELEBRATIONS

Each year, people from around the world visit New Orleans. Nearly 18 million people visited the city in 2017. People are drawn to the city's historic sites. They also come to take part in celebrations. One celebration New Orleans is known for is Carnival. This is a Christian season of feasting. Carnival is also celebrated in other countries that have large Catholic populations, such as Brazil. The Carnival season ends with a festival called Mardi Gras, or Fat Tuesday. This festival marks the beginning of Lent. Lent is a Christian religious period before the Easter holiday. In the weeks leading up to Mardi Gras, there are parades and balls throughout New Orleans. The parades are full of beautiful floats, marching bands, and dance groups. Non-Christian holidays and events are celebrated in the city too.

New Orleans is not as big as some other major US cities. But many people enjoy visiting the city for its history, cultures, and food. In these ways, New Orleans remains an iconic US city today.

CHAPTER
TWO

EARLY HISTORY

The first inhabitants of present-day Louisiana settled in the area approximately 12,000 years ago. They were Native Americans. They belonged to several tribes, including the Atakapa, Choctaw, Chitimacha, Natchez, and Tunica.

The first Europeans to explore the area were French fur trappers. They had settled there by the 1690s. French explorer René-Robert Cavelier, Sieur de La Salle arrived in the area in 1682. He called the region *Louisiane*, or "Louis's land." This name honored France's King Louis XIV.

A Choctaw Native American performs a traditional dance at the New Orleans Jazz & Heritage Festival in 2019.

Jean-Baptiste Le Moyne, Sieur de Bienville was the governor of Louisiana in the early 1700s.

French trappers traded animal furs with Native Americans in the area. Then in 1718, a group of French settlers founded a colony near the Mississippi River. The settlers called the colony *Nouvelle-Orléans*, or New Orleans.

The French settled along both sides of the Mississippi River because it was the highest ground. Much of the area was swampland. The settlers cleared the land so they could turn it into a city.

At first, the settlers had difficulties building up New Orleans. Between 1721 and 1722, two hurricanes hit the area. They destroyed much of the city. Even in good weather, the land was often muddy. It was difficult to build on this land.

After the hurricanes, French engineer Adrien de Pauger came up with a plan for the city. Pauger created a grid pattern with Saint Louis Cathedral in the center. This pattern is still visible in the French Quarter and other New Orleans neighborhoods today.

EXPANSION AND CHANGE

The first New Orleans residents came from a variety of backgrounds. Some were Native Americans. Others were French or Spanish. European settlers brought enslaved Africans to New Orleans. These enslaved people came from Africa and from colonies in the Caribbean.

New Orleans became the capital of the Louisiana Territory in 1722. The city's population continued to grow. It was a center for trade. Merchants sold items such as tobacco, rice, and vegetables.

THE REVOLUTIONARY WAR

New Orleans played a key role in the Revolutionary War (1775–1783). The Revolutionary War was a conflict between American colonists and Great Britain. The colonists lived in Great Britain's North American colonies. They wanted independence from British rule. New Orleans residents used the Mississippi River to ship weapons and money to the colonists. These materials helped the colonists win the war.

In the 1760s, the French did not think they were making enough money from New Orleans. They gave New Orleans and the rest of the Louisiana Territory to the Spanish in 1763 as part of the Treaty of Paris. The French residents eventually adapted to Spanish rule.

In 1788, a large fire swept through New Orleans. It destroyed nearly 80 percent of the city's buildings. After the fire, residents rebuilt and expanded the city. Many of the buildings in the French Quarter today date back to the Spanish period.

THE LOUISIANA PURCHASE

In 1800, Spain gave Louisiana back to France. But France did not hold on to the territory for long. In 1803, French ruler Napoleon Bonaparte sold the Louisiana Territory to the United States as part of the Louisiana Purchase. Then in 1812, the first state was carved from the territory. The state was called Louisiana.

New Orleans soon became a hub for trade in cotton

PERSPECTIVES
SELLING THE CITY

Before the Louisiana Purchase, New Orleans was the capital of the French territory in North America. The French settlers enjoyed the city's social life. There were places in the city where all classes of people could listen to music or watch dancing or fencing. But New Orleans did not make the French Empire much money. The French needed money to fight wars in Europe. So Bonaparte sold Louisiana to the United States. This land addition doubled the size of the country. President Thomas Jefferson saw the value of the land. He said, "The position of New Orleans certainly destines it to be the greatest city the world has ever seen."

THE
LOUISIANA
PURCHASE

This map shows the land the United States gained as part of the Louisiana Purchase. Modern state borders are also shown. The Louisiana Territory was 828,000 square miles (2.1 million sq km). What do you think were the benefits of having this new land?

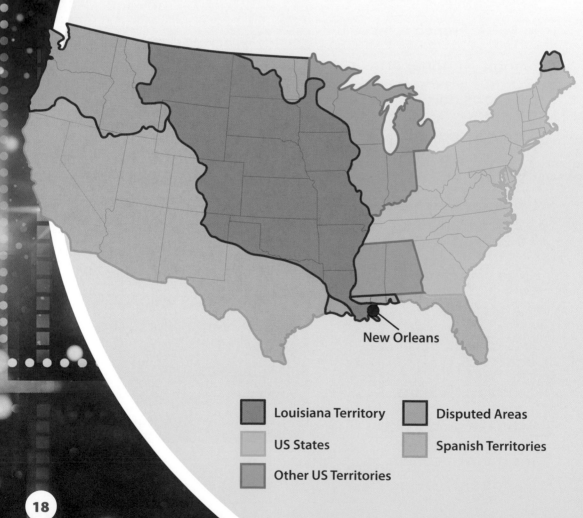

New Orleans

Louisiana Territory

US States

Other US Territories

Disputed Areas

Spanish Territories

and sugar. Steamboats transported goods along the Mississippi River. These goods went to places such as the Caribbean, South America, and Europe.

New Orleans also played a key role in the slave trade. Enslaved people were often separated from their families. Then they were brought into Louisiana through the city's port. They were forced to plant and harvest cotton and other crops on large farms called plantations. By 1820, New Orleans had become the largest slave market in the South.

EXPLORE ONLINE

Chapter Two talks about the early history of New Orleans. The article at the website below goes into more depth on this topic. As you know, every source is different. How is the information from the website the same as the information in Chapter Two? What new information did you learn?

HISTORY OF NEW ORLEANS

abdocorelibrary.com/new-orleans

CHAPTER
THREE

THE CIVIL WAR AND ITS AFTERMATH

I n the mid-1800s, many people disagreed on the issue of slavery. These disagreements divided the country. Many southerners defended slavery. They depended upon enslaved people to grow crops and do other skilled work. For example, enslaved people in New Orleans were forced to build levees. Southern slaveholders wanted to expand slavery into new territories. But some northerners opposed this. They wanted to end slavery or stop it from spreading.

Slaveholders made enslaved people build plantation houses such as the Nottoway mansion in Louisiana. Slaveholders lived in these houses.

The divisions between the states caused the country to split in 1861. Eleven southern states separated from the United States. They formed the Confederacy. Louisiana was part of the Confederacy. Northern states remained in the Union. Conflict broke out between the Union and the Confederacy. This conflict was called the American Civil War (1861–1865).

UNION RULE

In 1862, Union navy ships entered New Orleans from the Gulf of Mexico. The Union forces easily captured New Orleans. Union general Benjamin Butler took charge of New Orleans. The city remained under Union control until the end of the war.

Union leaders made positive changes to New Orleans. They improved the city's drainage systems to help prevent flooding. They also gave supplies and aid to poor residents. Unlike other southern cities, New Orleans was not damaged much during the war.

General Benjamin Butler was the military governor of New Orleans for eight months in 1862.

In 1863, President Abraham Lincoln signed the Emancipation Proclamation. This order freed enslaved people in the parts of the South that were still under Confederate control. Because New Orleans was under Union control, the order did not apply to enslaved people in New Orleans. But the presence of Union troops in the city encouraged many enslaved people to flee their slaveholders.

P. B. S. PINCHBACK

P. B. S. Pinchback was a black Union officer during the Civil War. He was elected to the Louisiana State Senate in 1868. He became Louisiana's governor in 1872. He was the first African American governor in the United States. He remained the governor until January 1873. In 1875, he ran for a spot in the US Congress. He won the most votes, but his opponent argued that the results were not valid. So his opponent took office. African American author James Haskins wrote, "Historians really do not know much about Pinchback . . . or for that matter, about any of yesterday's black public figures."

AFTER THE WAR

In January 1865, the Thirteenth Amendment passed. This amendment outlawed slavery in the United States. Then in April, the Civil War ended. The Union won the war.

Louisiana rejoined the Union in 1868. African Americans became US citizens. They gained some rights as citizens. For example, black men gained the right to vote. White southerners

In the early 1900s, many African Americans in Louisiana were low-paid sharecroppers. Sharecroppers rented land in exchange for part of the crop.

disliked this. They created laws that restricted black people's rights. In Louisiana and other parts of the South, lawmakers created barriers that kept black people from voting. African American men had to pay a tax or pass a difficult test in order to vote. White hate groups such as the Ku Klux Klan attacked African Americans. Their goal was to intimidate black people. New Orleans had a large black population in the 1870s.

PLESSY v. FERGUSON

In 1892, Homer Plessy boarded a train in New Orleans. He sat in a section that was designated for white people. He refused to get up and was arrested. Plessy brought his case to the US Supreme Court. His case was called *Plessy v. Ferguson.* Plessy's opponents argued that segregation in train cars was legal. They said there were an equal number of cars for black and white passengers. The Supreme Court agreed with the opposing side. It said that segregation was lawful as long as black and white people were treated equally. In reality, the facilities and services provided to black people were often worse than those provided to white people.

Black residents felt the effects of these attacks and restrictions.

SEGREGATION

Despite strides toward equality in the decades after the war, New Orleans and other southern cities became racially segregated. Racial segregation is the forced separation of people into groups based on their race. Black people were kept apart from white people in many ways. For example, they could not attend the same schools. Black New Orleans residents created organizations to fight segregation.

In the late 1800s, passenger-train cars in Louisiana were segregated. Trains needed to have separate sections for white and black passengers. The issue of segregation in New Orleans was brought to the national stage in 1892. In that year, Homer Plessy brought his case to the US Supreme Court. Plessy was a Creole resident of New Orleans. He had been arrested for riding in the white section of a train. He lost his case. But he inspired others to fight segregation.

FURTHER EVIDENCE

Chapter Three describes how the South was segregated in the late 1800s. What was one of the main points of the chapter? What evidence is included to support this point? Read the article at the website below. Does the information on the website support the point you identified? Does it present new evidence?

JIM CROW LAWS

abdocorelibrary.com/new-orleans

CHAPTER
FOUR

CHANGES AND CHALLENGES

I n the early 1900s, New Orleans faced some challenges. A large railroad system had been built throughout the South. Railroads connected the East and West Coasts. More people used trains instead of steamboats to transport goods. As a result, New Orleans's economy suffered.

During these difficult times, people sought out entertainment in the city. They flocked to clubs and dance halls. Musicians played jazz in these places. New Orleans jazz musicians such as pianist Jelly Roll Morton became popular

The first streetcars in New Orleans were created in the 1800s. Today, some streetcars still run through the city.

across the country. Jazz became part of a cultural movement in the 1920s. This era was known as the Jazz Age. People explored new styles of music and dance. New Orleans became known as the Birthplace of Jazz.

THE ORIGINS OF JAZZ

Musicians developed jazz music in New Orleans in the 1870s. But jazz did not become popular throughout the country until after 1900. Black musicians combined musical elements from different cultures to create jazz music. They were inspired by musical styles from Africa, the Caribbean, African American traditions, and Europe. Over the years, New Orleans continued to be famous for its jazz music. The musician perhaps best known for popularizing jazz was trumpeter Louis Armstrong. Armstrong was born in New Orleans. He was influenced by other New Orleans jazz musicians such as King Oliver.

MIGRATION AND THE DEPRESSION

Many African Americans left New Orleans in the early 1900s. They were part of the Great Migration. This was a mass movement of black people out of the South. Racial violence was common in

In the 1930s, many black workers built levees along the Mississippi River to prevent flooding.

the South. Black people wanted to escape this violence. They also hoped to find better job opportunities in other parts of the country. Many black New Orleans residents moved to the West Coast.

In the 1930s, many people across the country were out of work. They could not find jobs. This period was called the Great Depression. The US government developed a program called the Works Progress Administration (WPA). The WPA created jobs in construction and the arts. In New Orleans, WPA workers built many bridges and buildings.

CIVIL RIGHTS

Beginning in the 1930s, many white New Orleans residents moved out of the inner city. They settled in the surrounding suburbs. Developers who built these new suburbs prevented black families from buying homes there. This made New Orleans even more segregated. The population in the inner city was mostly black, while the suburban population was mostly white.

In the 1950s and 1960s, New Orleans played an important role in the American civil rights movement. Civil rights activists fought for racial equality. On November 14, 1960, six-year-old Ruby Bridges became the first black student to go to an all-white elementary school in the South. In 1954, the Supreme Court had made a major ruling in the case *Brown v. Board of*

US marshals escorted Ruby Bridges to and from school to protect her from angry and violent white protesters.

Education of Topeka. The court said school segregation was harmful to black students. The court ordered schools to integrate. All-white schools had to accept black students. Ruby attended William Frantz Elementary School in New Orleans.

Ruby's integration of William Frantz Elementary was the beginning of the end of segregation. The Civil Rights Act was later passed in 1964. The act outlawed segregation.

STRAIGHT TO THE
SOURCE

African American activist Jerome Smith was involved in the civil rights movement in the 1960s. Smith is from New Orleans. In 2011, he said of his activism:

> *Our people always put themselves up for struggle. Many of the unknown paid a tremendous price. It was all about our collective strength. The collective thing was much more powerful than . . . whatever my humble contributions were. . . .*
>
> *All the fear was never in the moment itself. It was always after, when you'd think about what you'd done, what you'd been through, and tremble. Most times I would try to deal with the moment with a kind of emotional detachment . . . because you cannot surrender. You have to keep moving forward.*

Source: Jerome Smith. "A Freedom Rider's First Stand." *AARP*. AARP, May 3, 2011. Web. Accessed August 1, 2019.

Consider Your Audience

Adapt this passage for a different audience, such as your friends. Write a blog post conveying this same information for the new audience. How does your post differ from the original text and why?

PICKING UP THE PIECES

New Orleans's tourism industry expanded throughout the late 1900s. Tourism boosted the city's economy. In 1970, the city hosted two big events. One of these events was the Super Bowl football championship. Another was the New Orleans Jazz & Heritage Festival. This was the city's first jazz festival.

The city's economy continued to grow throughout the 1990s. But in 2005, a major storm devastated the city. Hurricane Katrina hit New Orleans on August 29.

Jazz trumpeter Lionel Ferbos regularly performed at the New Orleans Jazz & Heritage Festival.

It brought rain and winds that traveled at speeds of more than 100 miles per hour (160 km/h).

Hurricanes are common in New Orleans because of the city's location near the Gulf of Mexico. People had built levees to protect the city. But when Katrina hit, some of the city's levees broke. As a result, 80 percent of the city flooded. Everyone who remained in the city needed to be evacuated, or moved to a safer place. New Orleans mayor Ray Nagin had urged people to leave the city ahead of the storm. But thousands of residents did not own cars and

PERSPECTIVES

WETLAND RESTORATION

Much of New Orleans is below sea level. This makes the city prone to flooding. Over the years, people destroyed many wetlands in New Orleans. Wetland destruction has made the flooding worse. Wetlands act like a sponge. They can hold a lot of water. Without wetlands, water can flow freely from the ocean into the city. Researchers say that it is important to restore wetlands to protect the city from future storms.

had no means of transportation. Many people took refuge in the Louisiana Superdome during the storm. The Superdome is a large football stadium in the city.

The hurricane killed more than 1,800 people. It destroyed many buildings and other structures. Thousands of people became homeless. Many moved out of the city. Others struggled to raise enough money to rebuild their homes.

It took days for the US government to provide aid. The city slowly recovered after Katrina. This recovery process took years. Many people believed the US government did not respond fast enough to the emergency. They think some lives could have been saved if the government had helped out sooner.

NEW ORLEANS TODAY

In 2006, the Superdome reopened. The professional football team the New Orleans Saints moved back to the city. Fans rejoiced as the Saints won their first game of 2006 in the Superdome. Fans also celebrated when

THE MUSICIAN'S VILLAGE

Singer Harry Connick Jr. and saxophonist Branford Marsalis both grew up in New Orleans. After Katrina, they planned a community of new homes and apartments for low-income residents. Volunteers began building this community in 2006. It is called the Musician's Village. People can study music, theater, and dance at the Ellis Marsalis Center for Music. The Musician's Village helped give the residents of New Orleans hope after the disaster.

the team won its first Super Bowl in 2010.

As the city recovered, attractions such as Mardi Gras and the Jazz & Heritage Festival drew in visitors from around the world. The city's tourism industry slowly grew. This helped the city make money as it continued to rebuild.

New Orleans and its residents have overcome many challenges. Today, the city is a popular destination for many travelers. They want to learn about the city's history and cultures. New Orleans remains a resilient and iconic American city.

STRAIGHT TO THE
SOURCE

Craig E. Colten is a professor of geography at Louisiana State University. He studied Hurricane Katrina's effects on black and low-income residents. In a 2005 interview, he said:

> *The wealthiest people [in New Orleans] have oftentimes lived on the highest areas in town, which are, in many cases, only 15 feet [5 m] or so above sea level. And that has left the least desirable locations to the people with the least means. . . .*

> *Many whites moved first to Jefferson Parish, the immediately upstream suburban parish during the 1950s and 1960s. They've been able to develop a fairly secure drainage system for themselves and [a] levee protection system. So . . . class and wealth do play a big part [in] people's ability to respond. And certainly, those people with the least means lose everything.*

> Source: "Race, Poverty and Katrina." *National Public Radio.* NPR, September 2, 2005. Web. Accessed August 1, 2019.

Back It Up

The author of this passage is using evidence to support a point. Write a paragraph describing the point the author is making. Then write down two or three pieces of evidence the author uses to make the point.

IMPORTANT
DATES

1718
French settlers found the city of New Orleans.

1763
France gives New Orleans to Spain through the Treaty of Paris.

1803
The United States gains the Louisiana Territory through the Louisiana Purchase.

1862
The Union army captures New Orleans during the Civil War.

1920s
Jazz music becomes widely popular. New Orleans becomes known as the Birthplace of Jazz.

November 14, 1960
Ruby Bridges becomes the first black student to attend an all-white elementary school in the South. She attends William Frantz Elementary School in New Orleans.

1970
New Orleans hosts its first Jazz & Heritage Festival.

2005
Hurricane Katrina hits New Orleans. It destroys much of the city. Thousands of people move out of the city.

STOP AND
THINK

Tell the Tale

Chapter One of this book describes a girl's trip through the French Quarter in New Orleans. Imagine you are making a similar journey. Write 200 words about your experience. What sites or landmarks are you excited to see? Why?

Surprise Me

Chapter Two discusses the early history of New Orleans. After reading this book, what two or three facts about this history did you find most surprising? Write a few sentences about each fact. Why did you find each fact surprising?

Dig Deeper

After reading this book, what questions do you still have about New Orleans? With an adult's help, find a few reliable sources that can help you answer your questions. Write a paragraph about what you learned.

Say What?

Studying a historic city such as New Orleans can mean learning a lot of new vocabulary. Find five words in this book you've never seen before. Use a dictionary to find out what they mean. Then write the meanings in your own words, and use each word in a new sentence.

GLOSSARY

colony
land owned by a faraway
nation or country

economy
a system in which goods and
services are exchanged

industry
a particular line of work

integrate
to bring different groups of
people together

levee
an earthen mound piled up
along the bank of a river or
lake to prevent flooding

parish
an area or district
in Louisiana

plantation
a large crop farm

segregation
the process of separating
people of different races or
ethnic groups

suburb
a community near a city

treaty
a formal agreement between
two or more groups

ONLINE RESOURCES

To learn more about New Orleans, visit our free resource websites below.

Visit **abdocorelibrary.com** or scan this QR code for free Common Core resources for teachers and students, including vetted activities, multimedia, and booklinks, for deeper subject comprehension.

Visit **abdobooklinks.com** or scan this QR code for free additional online weblinks for further learning. These links are routinely monitored and updated to provide the most current information available.

LEARN MORE

Huddleston, Emma. *The New Orleans Levee Failure*. Minneapolis, MN: Abdo Publishing, 2020.

Zullo, Allan. *Heroes of Hurricane Katrina*. New York: Scholastic, 2015.

INDEX

About the Author

Michael Decker has spent his career as a children's book author, writing about various topics. Decker has also spent more than a decade coaching youth sports. He lives in Laramie, Wyoming, with his wife, three kids, and his dog, Emily.